T0194075

Simply Read!

An innovative Way to Read with Fluency and Comprehension

How to quickly
transform a discouraged reader
into a proficient reader

VERA GOODMAN

EDITOR
Terry Davies

Order this book online at www.trafford.com
or email orders@trafford.com

Most Trafford titles are also available at major online book retailers.

Print information available on the last page.

ISBN: 978-1-6987-0002-1 (sc)
ISBN: 978-1-6987-0001-4 (hc)
ISBN: 978-1-6987-0044-1 (e)

Library of Congress Control Number: 2020906543

Design:
Ghaile Pocock, Bulldog Communication Inc.
Calgary, Alberta, Canada (403) 228-9861

Photography:
Trudie Lee Photography
Calgary, Alberta, Canada

Trafford rev. 04/03/2020

 www.trafford.com
North America & international
toll-free: 1 888 232 4444 (USA & Canada)
fax: 812 355 4082

*This book is dedicated
to the children and parents
who have been my teachers.*

Table of CONTENTS

Introduction **I**NTRODUCTION

As a **PARENT** *you have been cast in the* **ROLE** *of your child's most important* **TEACHER**. *Attitudes and values are contagious. They can inspire* **CONFIDENCE** *and a love of reading.*

Dialogue between adult and child is at the heart of successful reading.

Recently a mother phoned to thank me for my influence in her son Robin's life. I tutored Robin in grade two. He is now doing well in grade six and, best of all, he loves to read. In the course of our conversation his mother made a gratifying comment, "I realize now that fifty percent of what you did for Robin was in what you did for me. I was frustrated, worried and anxious. You helped me to relax and enjoy reading with my son. I let him develop at his own pace and it has really paid off."

Academic success is based on the ability to read. To help each of my students reach their potential, I decided early in my teaching career to become knowledgeable and competent in the field of reading instruction. Combining what I had learned from the work of others with my own observations, I set about doing classroom research. Later, as an administrator, I assisted in conducting research projects that proved to be unusually successful with children who were delayed in reading.

Reading can be learned through many different teaching methods. Regardless of how reading is being taught, the relationship between the coach and the reader as they practice together has a great impact, not only on learning to read, but on whether reading will be chosen as a pastime. In this book I provide simple, practical ideas that will help parents, reading volunteers and coaches to make the best use of time spent practicing.

I have spent hundreds of hours tutoring individual students and working with their parents. The reading philosophy presented here is based on lessons learned from these interactions and on twenty-seven years of teaching and learning with classes from grades one to nine.

Both parents and educators who know my work have urged me to write this book. It is meant to be a guide that you can read, digest and return to when necessary. I focus my writing on behaviors that affect what happens today, as you sit beside your child with a book to share. I do not want to present a yardstick by which to measure your past experiences.

No attempt is made to present a reading method or to provide a recipe for success. I simply share beliefs and strategies that have proven successful in my work with students over the years. Many discussions in the book are directed to the parents of children who are having trouble learning to read. I realize that the majority of children learn to read well and are anxious to read with their parents from the start. However, the approach to reading, and the activities presented in this book, will enrich the sharing time of all those who are helping others learn to read.

Some children have learning problems which make reading more difficult. They are in special need of coaching that shows them how to bring all their strengths to reading. It has been my experience that children will read more easily and with greater understanding if they are given strategies that support them in positive ways.

It is not always possible to help your own student. Emotions and conflicting expectations can get in the way. For a while, you may need to have your child read with someone else. But don't give up your sharing time. Enjoy books together. When they are ready, readers want to read to others.

I have dealt with many frustrated parents. One distraught mother told me she would ask herself, "What am I doing wrong? How am I failing? I've been a bad mother today, I haven't read with my child." It is natural and important to be concerned about your child's progress. I hope that the Reading Wings Approach to reading will let you relax and have fun learning together.

Simply Read! is a revision of my bestseller *Reading is More Than Phonics!* The chapter on adolescents and adults is added to this new version to show how this approach can be used to coach anyone who has not learned to read well. The new title fits with a series of *Simply* books I am writing on issues in education. The second book, *Simply Write!*, is now available. Its premise is that, just as families who read together give their children a head start on learning to read, families who model and celebrate writing together give their children an advantage in becoming effective writers.

Over the last few years the pendulum of public discussion around reading has swung in the direction of phonics instruction as the best way to achieve reading success. Although a knowledge of letters and their sounds is important, those who are learning to read need to be able to use their understanding of the subject matter to help them as they approach printed text. They also need positive support to build confidence.

My purpose is to put phonics into perspective. There are many factors that affect one's ability to read. Reading is more than phonics!

"It is not the bookish home, nor necessarily the middle-class family, not high intelligence, good eye movements, acute ears, nor even extensive vocabulary that makes the successful beginner. The supporting adult, who shows him what a book is and how print works, who helps him to discover reading and expects him to be successful, makes all the difference. Together, adult and child learn about reading."

Margaret Meek

Acknowledgements CREDITS

Who do you **ACKNOWLEDGE** *when there are so many who have* **INFLUENCED** *your ideas and your writing?*

Thanks to all the people who have enriched my life.

My success as a teacher has been fostered by years of watching master teachers practice their craft. My view of reading has been framed by studying the research of scholars in the field of literacy.

Margaret Meek, a noted British educator, has greatly influenced my understanding of reading and learning. The reading model in Chapter Two is based on her beliefs about how children learn to read. Listening to Humberto Maturana, a biologist from Chili, enhanced my understanding of life. This man's ability to simplify the complexities of everyday living enabled me to simplify my view of reading. The diagram in Chapter Three is an adaptation of his behavior model.

Several people reviewed my manuscript and gave me valuable feedback. Bernie and Jan McCaffery kept urging me to write this book so that other parents could share the insights they found valuable. Marg Edmonds prodded me to get started and encouraged me to keep writing. Rae Sharpe read my rough drafts many times and provided intellectual and emotional support.

The skillful editing of Terry Davies helped to clarify for others what was so obvious to me. Ghaile Pocock of Bulldog Communication created the unique design and layout of the book and cover. This look is now the basis of the visual brand for my series of educational books.

My grandchildren, Sean, Bryce and Rachel, keep me aware of the responsibility I have to encourage a new generation of readers.

How do Children LEARN?

I *am convinced that the* **EXPERIENCES** *of the child, the* **BEHAVIORS** *of the family and the* **EXPECTATIONS** *of the society in which they live are all part and parcel of* **LEARNING** *to* **READ.**

Reading goes beyond the printed page in many significant ways.

Reading skills are acquired as we read books, share experiences and engage in talk with children. Feelings, attitudes, beliefs and the climate within the family are all important. Children will pick up the view of reading presented by their first teachers, the family.

Family members who know a child and the experiences which have been part of the child's life are equipped to provide the support their young reader needs. Although it is possible for children to learn to read by reading only at school, most require extra practice.

Reading is learned through apprenticeship. Just as you cannot learn to drive a car by reading a book on how to drive a car, you cannot learn to read by reading a book on how to read. The art of reading is gained through guided practice.

How do humans learn? The most obvious ways that come to mind are memorizing, experiencing, practicing and listening. In our society, we often think of learning as being the result of formal education. However, much of what we learn happens without conscious awareness and many more subtle factors are involved.

The brain builds a pool of knowledge based on experiences encountered from moment to moment. We cannot stop ourselves from learning. However, what is learned may not be what we want to learn or what is being taught. For instance, it is possible that efforts to teach reading might result in some children learning to dislike reading.

CHILDREN LEARN FROM:

* experiencing success and failure
* being tested and labelled
* copying the behaviors of others
* taking risks and dealing with consequences
* interacting with peers
* listening in on adult conversations
* hearing and telling stories
* interpreting facial expressions and tone of voice
* being rewarded for behaviors
* and so on, and so on...

THE ROLE OF SELF-TALK

Individually, we make sense of experience by talking to ourselves in thought. In our self-talk, we make up conversations, relate new ideas to prior experiences, reflect on how our words and actions are received by others and plan future behaviors. It is the way we define who we are and how we view our world. The brain organizes these inputs into little worlds of experience which we use to make sense of our lives. We become the person we talk to ourselves about!

The difficulty with self-talk is that it is not necessarily true nor accurate. The comments, motives and attitudes encountered are often interpreted incorrectly as we think, reflect and react. Nevertheless, it all becomes part of the experience base which guides future decision-making and frames our view of life. It is possible for a child to talk himself out of reading!

Self-talk is the way in which children give themselves instructions. They actively create their own learning from the information they receive. The ability to learn effectively is determined by their emotional state and it is self-talk that determines how they feel.

Each family builds its own language of self-talk — talk that helps each individual either to maintain a positive self-image or to build feelings of incompetence and inferiority.

The ability to read well depends on the breadth of our experience. Children are in great need of extended discussion with adults on a variety of subjects. Through such dialogue they learn valuable thinking skills and recognize that they have opinions and ideas that are valued by others. Talking together about current events, history, science and other subjects builds academic confidence. A child cannot talk to himself about important and interesting topics if he has never been exposed to them.

One father I know reads the atlas with his pre-schoolers. He tells stories from various countries and points out interesting things about the physical world. They love it! He is instilling a lifelong interest in geography and history!

What kinds of things do you say in your child's hearing about reading, learning, teachers and school? Comments such as, "Your school library sure has a lot of interesting books we can share," and "You should hear the good story Jennifer can tell to accompany the pictures in this book," build positive images of reading and books. On the other hand, "Jennifer can't read, I don't know what we're going to do!" or, "Don't schools teach reading anymore?" undermine confidence.

A mother who was extremely worried because her seven-year-old son couldn't read yet told me that, out of frustration, she was saying things like, "You can't even read *the*, or *of*, or *from*! Those are baby words!" What a perfect way to reinforce his suspicion that reading is too hard for him!

You may have legitimate concerns about your child's progress or the ways in which she is being taught. Share these concerns with the teacher, not the child. If you discuss your frustrations about her reading with others, make sure she is not listening. Negative remarks have a very negative influence.

Humans seem to have an inborn ability to live up to labels and nicknames. The words you use to describe your child as a reader will have a strong effect on who she will become.

Confidence building is the key to reading success. The trick is to talk positively, to assure children we believe in them until they have had the time and experience to believe in themselves. For young children this involves keeping from them any hint that they might not become skillful readers.

Childhood is a fragile time. Confidence is a flame that can be extinguished by a little puff of doubt. Reading is especially subject to the winds of doubt. It involves risk-taking and beginners must see themselves as successful before they are capable. The learner must be invited, from the beginning, to behave like a reader. The kind of self-talk we want to cultivate is, "It's ok. It's a little tough, but I can do it!" I cannot stress too much the importance of maintaining this kind of confidence.

How many words do you have to read to be a reader? One! I let my beginners know this. An appropriate comment might be, "Look at that! You can read. If you can read one word, you can read thousands of words. You're a reader!" Children can label themselves 'Reader' early in life. This helps them to maintain a positive image of themselves as readers.

Attitude has a great influence on learning. Enjoyment and pleasure are transmitted quickly. So are frustration and disappointment. Children are often hard on themselves and can become discouraged easily. The emotional state of both you and your child influences sharing time. Because discouraged readers are often harder to get on track than beginners they, in particular, need your positive support and enthusiasm. Together you must build the confidence needed for successful reading.

Summary of Key POINTS

READING goes beyond the printed page. * Reading is learned through **GUIDED PRACTICE**. * There isn't **TIME** for enough practice at school. * Children learn by **TALKING** to themselves. * **DIALOGUE** on meaningful topics builds academic confidence. * Children can't talk about things they haven't yet **ENCOUNTERED**. * Maintaining confidence is the key to reading success. * Beginners must see themselves as successful before they are **CAPABLE**. * Negative **REMARKS** lead to negative self-talk. * Share your **CONCERNS** with the teacher — not the child.

Essentials for

LEARNING

to Read

To learn to read we need **FOUR** things, all of which are **INEXPENSIVE** and readily **AVAILABLE** — One who can **READ** — One who wants to **LEARN** — Time to **PRACTICE** — A selection of interesting **MATERIALS**.

It is not necessary to buy costly reading programs.

Those who want to learn to read can do so by reading with experienced readers. They need a variety of interesting reading materials, time to engage in conversations about their contents, and a reader to help them practice effectively.

Success in reading is directly related to the quality of dialogue engaged in by the reader and the learner. Reading is an active encounter between reader and print. Effective readers spend time mentally making connections and predicting both words and events. Beginners make these connections orally through conversation. Stop and talk about what you are reading. To create quality dialogue relate the story to personal experience, predict what will happen or question a point of view. Together you will discover the pleasures of reading. Shared reading time will be warm and special.

Only three things are needed to learn to read — interaction between an experienced reader and someone who wants to learn, and time to share interesting reading material.

One Who Can Read   **One Who Wants to Learn**

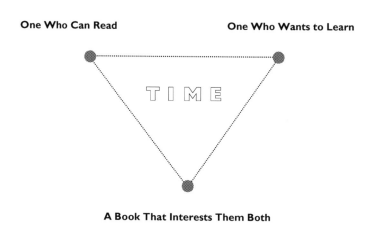

A Book That Interests Them Both

The reading material chosen is the key to quality dialogue. Something that appeals to the interests of both the experienced reader and the one who is learning will stimulate meaningful discussions.

ONE WHO CAN READ

That's you! Time constraints in schools are such that teachers cannot spend a lot of time reading with individual students. Family members or friends must be prepared to sit beside and help readers as they practice. Parents can do this well because they know their child's unique interests and experiences. They are also the child's most powerful role model.

The structures and guidelines children need in order to read successfully are taught at school. They are internalized through practicing at home.

Those of us who can read tend to forget that reading is a very personal experience. Society has arbitrarily set six as the age at which all children are expected to learn to read. By organizing children into grades based on age, we have set up an artificial system that expects children to march along as a group. Although everyone knows that this is unrealistic, change is difficult and we continue to put unnecessary pressure on beginners and on their teachers.

Labeling and sorting of students, based on the speed at which they progress in reading, begins in grade one. We foolishly impose standardized reading tests on children who we already know can't read independently. What an excellent way to destroy confidence and reinforce despair in those who are not yet ready to read!

Sometimes, as a result, children must repeat the entire year. The first grade child usually can't understand why he is being left behind because he feels he has done his best. And reading gets the blame.

Two stories of children I have known serve to illustrate this point. One little fellow who was not reading by the middle of grade one said to his grandma, "The other kids are away up there and I'm down here and we're getting farther apart. I'm stupid! I hate reading!"

Another boy who was informed that he had to repeat grade one because he hadn't learned to read said to his mother through his tears, "But they didn't teach me!" Both boys are bright and obviously they had both been taught along with the others. They both felt they were doing their best.

Not every seed produces a flower in the same number of days nor does every child learn to read independently on the same schedule. Why can't we accept this and let everyone produce flowers in their own time? We accept it for walking and talking so why should reading be any different? As we teach, support and encourage a beginner we must also trust him to set his own pace. This may be difficult to do when children are tested and labelled too early.

Let's hope that someone doesn't come up with a magic age at which infants must walk and talk or we will have to set up schools for remedial walking and talking!

Until a child has achieved some fluency in reading, it will be difficult to read alone and he should not be asked to do so. It is like learning to walk. We must be prepared to hold a child's hand until he signals that he's ready to try it alone by pulling his hand away — no matter how long that takes!

Letting children learn at their own pace does not mean forsaking standards and expectations. As reading processes are taught and reinforced, children must be challenged to improve their performance. The role of the teacher is to teach the skills needed for reading, to provide new experiences and to monitor progress.

Your most important contribution as a parent is to provide a warm supportive atmosphere, time for sharing, lots of patience, and a supply of appropriate material.

ONE WHO WANTS TO LEARN

No one really knows why reading comes so easily to some children while for others progress is slow. What we do know is that every child who enters grade one not only wants to learn to read but expects to do so. If they do not see themselves as readers fairly quickly, children can get turned off before they have given themselves a chance. They may say to themselves, "I don't want to read! I hate reading! I'm dumb!"

How do children judge their own progress? They might very well compare themselves to the best readers in the class. In many first-grade classes there are children who begin the year already reading independently. There are others who learn to read quickly and are able to join the ranks of those who are members of an exclusive club, the club of readers.

Those who are not yet reading want very much to belong to the club. In spite of what they say, all children want to read. Fear that they will never be able to master what others seem to be doing so easily leads to discouragement. Young children lack the maturity to realize their uniqueness. Moreover, everyone around them is expecting them to read.

The next step for some children is to avoid reading except when required to do so. They especially don't want to fail before family members, so they are reluctant to read at home. But reading and hockey have a lot in common — if you don't attend the practices you are not likely to make the team!

Books and reading must be seen to be both pleasurable and attainable or the learner will become discouraged. A discouraged child may not want to spend the time with books that is needed for mastery. Children must find in books human experiences with which they can identify. Don't tell a young child how important reading is, just help him to discover the fun of it.

Whether or not a child becomes an independent reader in grade one is not important. The image that he builds of himself as a reader and learner is critical.

TIME

Time is the coin we have to spend. Both the reader and the learner must agree to spend time together. As we deal with the stresses in our busy lives, time is a most difficult thing to find.

When you have a young child who is not yet reading independently, plan both your own and your child's activities so that you have blocks of time for exploring books together in a leisurely way. Keep extracurricular activities to a minimum for a while. Too much activity means that reading has to be squeezed in, often when everyone is overtired.

How we choose to spend our time sends a powerful message about what we value. My experience with Troy's family serves as an example. Both mom and dad worked, so time to spend together was at a premium. Reading was done as homework, sandwiched between baseball, swimming and a host of other activities. Mom assumed responsibility for reading with Troy. Dad taught him hobbies and helped him to achieve success in athletic events.

Troy was often tired when he came to read with me. He said he didn't like reading. Dad and mom assured me that they thought learning to read was important. I'm not sure that the way they were using their time gave that message to Troy.

The family planned together and rearranged their days. Dad and Troy made time to share books and magazines about baseball and other common interests. They began to enjoy learning together. They even found new ways to improve Troy's athletic skills through the books they read! As mom and dad shared different kinds of reading material with Troy his pool of knowledge was greatly enriched. It took time, but he is now a successful reader.

The world will not come to an end if you don't read every day. When it comes to reading time, quality is more important than quantity. Short sessions that inspire warm feelings towards books and reading can be balanced off with longer stretches that are more challenging. Relaxed sharing is the goal.

BOOKS

The books you choose to share will make all the difference. Select books on subjects that both you and your reader enjoy. Interesting books make for an interested reader! I have actually heard people say, "It doesn't matter what children read as long as they are reading." This makes as much sense as saying, "It doesn't matter what children eat as long as they are eating!"

Choice of reading material is so important that I have reserved a separate section for its consideration. If the material is too easy you will not be able to use this approach to reading. In Chapter Seven we look at why the choice of book influences the reading process and how to choose reading material that is appropriate for your child.

Summary of Key POINTS

Children **WANT** to read and **EXPECT** to learn. ❀ *Fear of failure undermines* **CONFIDENCE**. ❀ *Sharing times should be both* **FUN** *and* **CHALLENGING**. ❀ *Stop and* **TALK** *together as you read.* ❀ *Don't ask children to read aloud to others until they feel* **COMFORTABLE**. ❀ **CULTIVATE** *your child's interest and your flower will bloom in its own time.* ❀ *Have patience, but continue to actively tend your reader with* **GOOD TEACHING**.

Phonics and
EXPERIENCE

Building a **BRIDGE** *between the written word and the reader's unique* **EXPERIENCE** *is essential for* **READING.**

Reading is the result of blending print with experience.

To read, we must have a printed text. This can take many different forms such as words, sentences, pictures, charts and diagrams.

Experience, housed invisibly in the mind, is what the individual reader brings to print. Experience encompasses the information that can be recalled consciously as well as all the beliefs, attitudes and understandings in our subconscious pool of knowledge.

Phonics is the study of sounds and letters and how they relate to each other to make words. It is an important part of being able to read words in printed text. For many, phonics is considered to be the most important part of learning to read. Phonics programs are easy to teach and phonics knowledge is easy to test. It may appear logical that if one knows the sounds of letters and their combinations, reading will be easy.

My experience tells me that this is not necessarily true. I meet people who have been exposed to heavy doses of instruction in phonics and it has made them slow, ineffective readers.

We hear a lot today about going back to the basics or getting back to the good old days... whenever they were! As I talk with some who advocate this journey into the past, I find they are referring mainly to teaching reading through phonics.

"Well, I learned to read through phonics," they will say to me. Or, "I didn't learn to read well because they were using the sight method."

"You mean you sat in grade one and kept track of all the ways in which you were being taught to read?" I ask.

"Well, of course I couldn't do that!" they respond, realizing how impossible this would be.

"Then maybe you don't remember all the things that influenced your development as a reader," I conclude.

I decided to look through old readers and teaching guides to discover for myself what the basics might have been in the good old days. In the Alberta Program of Studies for 1942, I found this interesting advice to teachers:

"Please teacher, don't teach the beginner to read by the phonics method. This method is long out-of-date. It is based on the idea that in reading, the reader moves his eyes from one letter to the next, sounding out the word. A good reader does not move his eyes in this way and no child should have this bad habit fixed upon him. It makes his reading slower in speed and poorer in comprehension."

While writing this book, I had the good fortune to be reunited with the teacher who taught me to read and who instilled in me a lifelong love of learning. To me, Margaret Elliott was an angel in disguise when she came to our small town in southern Saskatchewan fresh from Normal School. For over 50 years I have treasured her in my thoughts. It was a dream come true to meet her again after all these years. Grade one teachers are special!

My curiosity about how reading was taught in the past prompted me to ask her what reading method she used in teaching us to read. She replied, "We were trained to teach you to read in whole words and sentences but not to break the words up into little parts!" It seems that in those good old days, phonics was not the first step in learning to read!

THE RELATIONSHIP OF PRINT TO EXPERIENCE

There should be no conflict between the roles of phonics and experience. Without a knowledge of letters, reading is impossible. If phonics training was not important, we would all be able to read solely on the basis of experience. It is equally clear that without experience it is impossible to read with understanding. Making sense out of print is what reading is all about.

One thing has become evident to me over the years. A reader needs to develop a feel for the reading experience before he begins to concentrate his efforts on decoding individual words. Many of the problem readers that I have worked with have the same definition of reading: sounding out words. When they view reading in this way their focus is on letters and individual words. There are many ways to approach reading, but readers who are intent on sounding out are unable to take advantage of their knowledge of the subject to read quickly and with comprehension. Attention must be shifted to the meaning.

Reading is making sense of print. We must utilize all our abilities while reading. Learners must be made to realize how much they already know that can help them to read. We need to show them how to use their pool of knowledge to unlock the mystery of print.

I am concerned when students label themselves by saying, "I have dyslexia," or some other learning disorder. If they feel they have a condition that is beyond their control, they can lose confidence in their own abilities. By taking on such a label, they may feel unable to learn by themselves and look to someone else to rescue them. Reading takes place in individual minds. No one else can do it for them.

I find that once someone has assumed a label, it is difficult to develop the confidence needed to read alone. Learning difficulties should be discussed among parents, teachers and specialists. Together they can plan appropriate strategies that will enable the child to rediscover the joy of learning. Children do not need to know the labels.

Most of the parents I talk to have one phrase they use most often as they help their children practice, "Sound it out!" This reflects an emphasis solely on phonics and does not offer any other approaches. Efficient readers must go beyond phonics. Successful reading is finding a happy balance between phonics and experience. The purpose of this book is to help you find that balance. The next chapter contains activities that demonstrate more clearly how readers can use their experience to make sense of the printed word.

Summary of Key POINTS

There is more to reading than **PHONICS**. ◈ Reading is **BLENDING** print with experience. ◈ There should be no conflict between the **ROLES** of phonics and experience in reading. ◈ When we give people a **LABEL** they may live up to it. ◈ We must help others to **RECOGNIZE** and use all their capabilities as they read. ◈ Making sense of **PRINT** is what reading is all about.

Reading with
UNDERSTANDING

Bringing **EXPERIENCE** *to print is more important to becoming a* **COMPETENT** *reader than is a* **KNOWLEDGE** *of phonics.*

Sounding out is difficult for beginning and discouraged readers.

To appreciate how hard it is to read by sounding out, I would like you to do the following activities. In a workshop some years ago, I was impressed by the way this exercise helped me put phonics and experience into perspective.

Read the following words. They are phonetically correct, but are spelled differently from the way you have learned them. You will find this assignment challenging but don't worry, so does everyone else!

vury	sctraugh
mould	sought
whoamb	phyue
dauss	ceokn
whir	pneocquez

Did you find it impossible, as I did, to read this list with certainty? If you feel frustrated, you may be experiencing the same emotions as your beginning reader when he is asked to sound it out or to read words from word lists.

Each word has a number of different possibilities, doesn't it? For instance, is *sc* pronounced *sk* or *s*? Even if we could recall all the ways sounds are represented in print we would still not know which to use.

Here is a story about baby robins. It contains the words you have just attempted to read from the list. If you have trouble with a word, look away from it and use your experience to think of what word would make sense.

"I am working vury hard," said the robin. "I am looking for sctraugh to build my nest. I shall use some mould, too. I shall line it with sought grass. This will make a nice whoamb for my baby birds." So she made the nest in the old apple tree. In a phyue dauss there were three little eggs in the nest. Ceokn there whir three baby robins. They stretched their little pneocquez and cried, "Peep, peep, feed us!"

Still rather difficult? But you were probably able to figure out most of the words and with a couple of re-readings you will be able to read the whole passage. Your understanding of the subject helps to limit the possibilities. It makes it easier to decode the unfamiliar words.

Look at this sentence as an example: "I shall use some mould too." In my workshops, some of those who read this say the word that means green fuzzy stuff on bread and just keep on reading. But when I stop and ask, "Does that fit with your knowledge of robin's nests?" they soon change the word to *mud* which is what birds use to build nests.

When you have figured out the words from context, go back and read the word list. It is quite easy now, isn't it?

Which helped you the most in reading the passage, phonics or experience? Your experience with robins provided you with the understanding necessary to figure out the words.

Learning all the sounds and their combinations and trying to use them in words can be a difficult and frustrating task. As you experienced by working through this exercise, too much focus on phonics makes reading more difficult.

Another passage that I was given to read in a workshop also illustrates the role that experience plays in reading.

The procedure is actually quite simple. First you arrange things into different groups. One pile may be sufficient depending on how much there is to do. It is important not to overdo things. That is, it is better to do too few things at one time than too many. In the short run, this may not seem important but complications can easily arise. A mistake can be expensive as well. At first, the whole procedure will seem complicated. Soon, however, it will become just another fact of life. After the procedure is completed, one arranges the materials into different groups again. Then they can be put into their appropriate places.

Did you have trouble reading this paragraph? Not likely. Did you understand what you read? Probably not. Why does it not make sense?

If I tell you that this paragraph is about doing laundry, you can read it with perfect understanding, can't you? Your brain now knows which world of experience to call on to structure meaning.

How literate are you? Although I read widely and have attended university for seven years, I am still illiterate! I am illiterate in a great many printed texts — computer handbooks, electricians' guides, lawyers' textbooks, mechanics' manuals, geological manuscripts and medical journals, to name only a few.

Recently, I picked up a copy of a newspaper that is published for truckers who drive large transports across North America. I was surprised to find that I couldn't understand some of the articles. I have no knowledge of words that are specific to the world of transportation. Furthermore, I couldn't read some of the words! I had not heard them spoken and I didn't know for sure what sounds the letters made or which syllable to accent.

We are only literate in material for which we have some frame of reference, some level of experience. To understand words we must understand the world in which the words are being used. This is fundamental to the ability to read.

Yet children are often expected to read whatever is presented to them even though their background of experience is more limited than ours. An example of this problem is standardized reading tests in which passages reflect different fields of knowledge and sometimes even different cultures. The results from such tests are often treated seriously and used as a basis for labelling and sorting children. No wonder some get stressed and discouraged!

CONSONANTS AND VOWELS

You may find reading the following passage a challenge at first, but I hope it will get easier as you go along.

This segment is taken from a book called *The Rainbow Goblins*. The Color Goblins are making plans to steal the Rainbow.

The Rainbow Goblins

The_ g_bl_ns c__ld h_rdly c_nt__n th__r _xc_t_m_nt. "S__n _ll th_ c_l__rs _f th_ R__nb_w w_ll b_ __rs," Y_ll_w gl__t_d.

W_'ll sn_tch _t _s _t r_s_s," s__d Gr__n, "wh_n th_ c_l__rs _r_ st_ll fr_sh _nd cr__my."

Not too hard? Now try this one:

```
_ _e   _o_ _i_ _   _ou_ _   _a_ _ _ _   _o_ _ai_   _ _ei_
e_ _i_e_e_ _.   "_oo_  _ll  _ _e  _o_o_ _ _  _f  _ _e  _ai_ _o_
_i_ _  _e  ou_ _,"  _e_ _o_   _ _oa_e_ .
```

Impossible? Right! The first passage contains only consonants and the second, vowels. These passages illustrate that the most important clues are in consonants. Consonants seem to be more consistent than vowels and beginners find them much easier to use.

You will notice that children use consonants when they begin to write with letters. They seem to have more difficulty isolating vowel sounds than consonant sounds. Vowels are often irregular and cause the most trouble when figuring out words. Isn't it fortunate that children can get on with reading before they have learned all the vowel rules and sounds!

Compare another sentence from *The Rainbow Goblins* represented in two different ways.

```
The_   gob_ _ _   swu_ _   thei_   lass_ _ _   ar_ _ _ _   and
ar_ _ _ _   and  hur_ _ _   th_ _   in_ _   the  sk_.
```

                                   and

```
_ _e   _ _ _ _ins   _ _ _ng   _ _eir   _ _ _ _oos   _ _ _ _nd   and
_ _ _ _nd  and  _ _ _led  _ _em  _ _to  the  _ _y
```

The first passage is quite easy, isn't it? The second is impossible. The beginnings of words contain the most important phonetic clues. Sometimes you do not have to look at the whole word because the initial sound triggers a word to fit the context. You can quickly check the rest of the word and go on.

Poor readers are often inefficient because they have been taught to look too carefully at each word. I help students to break this habit. Slow reading results in poor comprehension because the reader is so focused on individual words that he forgets what came before and has to re-read. For these children, reading is not enjoyable and so they avoid the practice needed to improve.

Reading does involve blending sounds together and sounding out, but the goal is to identify words using as few letters as possible. Effective readers depend less and less on analyzing all the parts and use consonants to make sensible predictions.

READING WITHOUT FORMAL INSTRUCTION

We have learned a great deal about reading from the research carried out with children who have learned to read without any direct instruction, sometimes at very early ages. For these children, there were no rules that needed to be learned. This may also be the case for those who read early in grade one. They have not had time to learn all the rules. Those who read well go beyond rules. They use their understanding to make sense.

I have worked with young children who read novels, but have a limited ability to hear individual sounds within words and are unable to spell with much success. Nicholas is a bright boy who had great difficulty reading simple grade one material. His mother told me that in grade two he suddenly started to read *Star Trek* novels on his own. He came to me for tutoring in spelling. I asked, "How do you read? I know you don't sound out all the letters in a word because you don't know your short vowels and you have difficulty hearing some of the consonants."

Nicholas looked up at me with a twinkle in his eye and a big smile on his face and said, "I only look at the beginnings and the ends."

I hugged him! "You have discovered the secret of reading. Now I will teach you to hear the sounds you need to learn to spell!" How fortunate for Nicholas that he wasn't handicapped by too much phonics before he learned to read! This is especially good news in a society where we expect children to read before many of them can isolate sounds or memorize rules.

Summary of Key POINTS

We are only **LITERATE** *in material with which we have some level of* **EXPERIENCE**. ❈ *Sounding out is not only* **DIFFICULT**, *it is often impossible.* ❈ *The most important clues are in the* **CONSONANTS**. ❈ *Too much focus on phonics* **COMPLICATES** *reading.* ❈ *Efficient readers depend less and less on the* **SOUNDS** *within individual words.*

Spelling and
SIGHT **W**ORDS

Spelling should never be **CONFUSED** *with reading.*

Although there are ways in which reading and

spelling **SUPPORT** *each other, they are opposite*

SKILLS*. Spelling translates sounds to* **LETTERS***,*

reading turns letters into **SOUNDS***.*

Stimulate interest in words by playing with them.

Reading is a creative art that involves blending ideas, discovering information and drawing conclusions. Correct spelling cannot be creative. It is standard in form with no room for individual interpretation. It is difficult and inconsistent.

Reading and spelling should complement each other. Children are fascinated by rhymes and jingles. They chant together as they skip. Refrains that are repeated in stories are quickly learned and imitated. Children like to play with words that rhyme. Spelling these words is a good way to begin learning phonics.

Phonics is the study of how letters combine to make speech sounds. Familiarity with letter groups such as *ing,* and *ight,* can help children to recognize words more quickly. Spelling lessons are ideal for teaching phonics. The combinations learned become part of the child's pool of knowledge. They are then recognized more quickly and easily during reading.

Through reading some people develop a sense for correctness that makes them good spellers. Others become excellent readers and never learn to spell well.

I want to caution parents not to get anxious about spelling too soon. Children go through a series of stages as they learn to spell just as they do learning to talk. Early emphasis on rules can be confusing. The reality is, English is a highly irregular language!

Confidence is needed for spelling just as much as it is for reading. An interest in books is critical to reading. An interest in words is basic to spelling. Talk informally to your child about words and how they are constructed. Spelling out names on cereal boxes when you are shopping and noticing signs while driving are examples of ways to draw attention to spelling and to have fun with words.

When stories come home from school, discuss the content but don't draw attention to spelling errors. Accept phonetic spelling, a child's best attempt to put down what he hears. Children first need to gain confidence in their ability to write interesting stories.

Being able to spell correctly is important. Your child will be better able to take advantage of spelling instruction in school if he develops confidence and a positive attitude toward spelling at home. Unless children are interested in words and in spelling them correctly they may not put out the effort required to become good spellers.

THE USE OF SIGHT WORDS

Beginning readers should not be given too many sight words to memorize out of context. It is a difficult task for some children to read words in isolation. Often words that are read easily in a story are not recognized on a word list. However, words that become familiar through repetition while reading will be easier to recognize by themselves.

A mother in one of my workshops expressed frustration with trying to teach her daughter to identify fifty sight words. She was expected to spell them, too! Lisa was in grade two and was not yet reading independently. Reading time became a struggle and Lisa didn't want to read with her mother anymore. The quality of their relationship, so important to confidence, was suffering.

If a child brings home word lists to memorize before he can read, use them to make up crazy stories or poems. Find the words in magazines and circle them with a marker. Put them on cards and play a game. Children learn very well through play.

Was and *saw* are examples of words that beginning readers often confuse. Most children mix them up at one time or another. They are really only a problem for children focused on sounding out. A reader who is concentrating on meaning will stop when he says the wrong word. For example, *I was a cow* and *I saw a cow* are quite different. Is it important at this stage to be able to read *was* and *saw* out of context? I don't think so.

SOMETIMES IT'S OK TO BE WRONG

In the beginning, don't correct words that are wrong if they still make sense. An example is substituting house for home. You want to emphasize the message that reading is making sense. However, do not allow wild guessing — saying any old word just to keep going. When this happens, stop and say, "Does that make sense? Listen!" Repeat the sentence the way it was read. Ask the child why it does not make sense and then figure out the correct word together. Or, after the child has identified the error, just give the right word and carry on to maintain fluency.

One mother told me that her son said "doo-dat-da-doo-wa" for "I want a drink of water". The family accepted the approximation and gave him a drink. In a spirit of fun, they asked each other for water in the same way. Everyone praised his attempts to communicate. They gave him as much time as he needed to speak correctly. This same spirit of fun and support must be maintained while children learn to read and spell.

The following poem demonstrates the complexities of spelling and the difficulties of using phonics to decode words.

ENGLISH

I take it you already know
Of tough and bough and cough and dough?
Others may stumble, but not you
On hiccough, thorough, slough and through?
Well done! And now you wish perhaps,
To learn of less familiar traps.

Beware of heard, a dreadful word
That looks like beard and sounds like bird
And dead: it's said like bed, not bead —
For goodness sake, don't call it deed!
Watch out for meat, and great and threat,
(They rhyme with suite and straight and debt).
A moth is not a moth in mother
Nor both in bother, broth in brother.

And here is not a match for there,
And dear and fear for bear and pear,
And then there's dose and rose and lose —
Just look them up — and goose and choose,
And cork and work and card and ward,
And font and front and word and sword,
And do and go, and thwart and cart —
Come, come, I've hardly made a start!

A dreadful language? Why, man alive!
I'd learned to talk it when I was five,
And yet to write it, the more I tried,
I hadn't learned it at fifty-five.

T.S. Watt   — in the *Manchester Guardian*

Summary of **K**ey **POINTS**

Spelling and reading are **DIFFERENT** *skills.* ✽
Spelling correctly is **IMPORTANT** *for older
students.* ✽ *Support your child's* **DEVELOPMENT**
as a **SPELLER** *just as you did as a speaker.*
✽ *Do not emphasize word lists until your
child has some* **SUCCESS** *in reading.* ✽
PRACTICE *words that are difficult by creating
games to* **PLAY** *with them.*

Instructive
FEEDBACK

Your **EFFECTIVENESS** *as a reading coach is enhanced when* **FEEDBACK** *on a child's reading* **IDENTIFIES** *helpful strategies and behaviors.*

Responses should strengthen skills and build confidence.

Reading coaches sometimes focus too much on the text and on getting it just right. The emphasis should be on making sense. Treat errors lightly to keep meaning flowing. Use difficult passages as opportunities to teach and reinforce effective behaviors. Knowing that it is ok to make mistakes lets a reader relax and read more naturally.

STRATEGIES FOR PRACTICING TOGETHER

The following are ways to support your reader, add variety to your sharing time and build reading skills.

Spend a lot of time reading out loud together, in chorus. Stay just a little behind to give your learner the first chance, but come in fairly quickly to keep the meaning flowing. You'll get used to this with practice. Sometimes, just whispering the beginning sound softly is the only cue that is necessary to trigger a word that makes sense. Stop on long words and demonstrate how to blend the consonants.

▭ Take turns reading pages, paragraphs or sentences. If the material is difficult, you might read a page and the child will read only a sentence. Model expressive reading and ask your reader to use her voice to communicate meaning and feeling, as if to an audience.

▭ Sometimes it is valuable to read aloud the entire book, page or paragraph before the child attempts it. Pause to explain new words and ideas. This builds background information. You will be surprised at how quickly readers become successful when they have an understanding of the message.

▭ When an error is made, it is often wise to wait until the end of the sentence before drawing attention to the mistake. A suitable comment would then be, "Did you understand that? It didn't make sense to me because I heard . . . . . Is that what you heard?" Figure out the word together and re-read the sentence. Discuss phonics as much as you like at this point because you have emphasized meaning first. When a reader begins to stop on his own because it doesn't make sense, you know he is making good progress.

▭ If a child is struggling with a word you know he has heard before, tell him to leave it out and finish the sentence. Re-read the sentence aloud leaving out the word. Often the right word will pop into his head. Emphasize reading with consonants and predicting from the letter or blend of letters at the beginning of a word. Be generous. Don't feel guilty about telling him the word if he is struggling. This is not a contest! It is important that fluency and confidence are maintained. If a word is unfamiliar, explain what it means.

▭ A sure way to build confidence is to help your reader master a bit of difficult material. Say, "I will read a paragraph and I want you tell me what it says. Then we'll read it together and figure out all the words you don't know. With a few practices, you will probably be able to read it by yourself even though it's pretty hard!"

▭ I like to use non-fiction for practice sessions. Books in the format of the *Eyewitness* series are ideal. Each page is a different aspect of the main topic. Read a whole section aloud, stopping to discuss new ideas and unfamiliar words. Pick a paragraph to work on. Read it together the first time through. Then ask your reader to read it again as quickly as possible while you use a watch to time the reading. Be generous. Give any words he stumbles on to keep him moving on. Have him re-read the passage until it is smooth. Record his progress by timing each attempt. The readers I work with enjoy this challenge and it gives practice in taking only minimal clues from the text. Occasionally, tape the second reading and the last one. Hearing oneself read fluently is critical to becoming a strong reader and is a great confidence builder.

▭ Pick a book you have already read together and ask your child to read it aloud while you are busy doing something else close by. When he needs a word, either pop over and give it to him or have him tell you the consonants. This is a great way to get independent reading started.

▭ A fun way to practice simple combinations such as *ing* or *ight* is to make up silly rhymes using as many rhyming words as possible. Or, use a colored marker to circle all the *ing* words on the page of a newspaper or a magazine. This is also an excellent way to practice recognition of individual letters if that is still a problem.

▭ It is helpful for beginners to know four consonant pairs that together make a different sound than each letter by itself: *ch th wh sh*. It is difficult to use the right clue when the reader thinks the word starts with *s* instead of *sh*.

▭ Look for chances to catch your reader doing something right. Tell her about it. Positive feedback is a powerful reinforcer. It lets the reader know you are paying attention. It identifies the behaviors that promote effective reading. It fosters the kind of self-talk that enables her to see her own success and to realize that she can do it on her own.

REPLACE "SOUND IT OUT"

- "Trouble with that word? Let's leave it out and finish the sentence. I bet it will pop into your head. Sometimes we don't know what word will make sense until we hear the rest of the sentence."

- "Let's put the beginning and ending sounds together," or, "That's a long word. We need to look at the middle consonants as well."

- "Look at me and tell me what word that starts with *sh* would make sense in this sentence. I'll repeat the sentence and you put in the word for me. *Shout!* See, you have to use your head and your eyes to read. Good work!"

- "That's a word that tells you how horses run. They *ga....* Yes, they gallop around the pasture."

- "This word is made of two other words which each has its own meaning. *Greenhouse* is a house for green plants."

- "We can't always depend on sounds being what we think they should be. *Ch* usually sounds like it does in *choo-choo* but in this word *chorus* it has a *k* sound so we have to look at the other letters in the word. We can use our heads to think of what would make sense or ask someone for help."

- "I'm going to cover this word and I'll bet, without even seeing it, you can tell me what it is when you read the sentence!"

- "Good reading! That's exactly what you should do. You're really getting the idea, aren't you."

FOCUS ON THE POSITIVE

- "I like the way you recognized that long word so quickly. How did you do it?"

- "I like the way you put the beginning, middle and end sounds together and said that word without sounding out each letter."

- "I like the way you stopped reading when that sentence didn't make sense."

- "I like the way you used the beginning sound to put in a word that fit."

- "I like the way you can tell me the meaning of new words by how they are used in the story."

- "I like the way you said that part. It sounded just like how Red Riding Hood would probably talk to the wolf."

- "I like the way you made a movie of the story in your head so you could retell it so well."

- "I like the book you brought home for us to share. I didn't know that eels always go back to the Sargasso Sea to spawn."

- "I like the way you take those Franklin books and read them by yourself after we have shared them. You really enjoy that series, don't you?"

- "I like the way you told the story of *Tom Thumb* to Grandpa. You must have really listened to the details when we read it."

It is important that the kind of responses and feedback illustrated in these charts be a part of reading right from the beginning. Regardless of the teaching methods employed at school, use these strategies when reading at home.

Children who fail to learn quickly are sometimes tested and labeled. Unfortunately, they often live up to the label they are given. Both their own self-talk and the names they are called by others reinforce the belief that they are not normal.

Children hate being singled out. They want to be accepted as part of the group. Making them feel different not only affects reading but it destroys the confidence they need to learn other things as well. Feeling inferior can lead to behavior problems.

Those who fail to keep up with what is considered normal for their age are sometimes slotted into structured programs based on phonics instruction. Worksheets and reading exercises are assigned. Drills are conducted on sounds and blends. Errors are pointed out on a regular basis. Discouragement is built into every wrong response.

This kind of teaching doesn't provide opportunities for students to take advantage of their unique experiences and learning styles. Those with difficulties don't always need more phonics. They often need reassurance that they are capable, confidence in their ability to learn in the same way as everyone else, good literature to read, and enjoyable practice with a knowledgeable coach.

The plight of Scarecrow in *The Wizard of Oz* is similar to that of many who struggle with reading. Scarecrow wanted a brain. He travelled to the Wizard expecting him to use his wizardry to replace the straw in his head. The Wizard knew there was no magic cure. He sent Scarecrow to kill the Wicked Witch, a task that would require all his skills. When his friends were under attack, Scarecrow thought of a plan that saved their lives. He went on to become the ruler of Emerald City. He found his brain by using it!

Young readers need to discover and use their abilities. They do this best by reading, not by doing exercises about reading!

Summary of Key POINTS

Feedback should **IDENTIFY** *the strategies you want your reader to use.* ◦ *Take turns reading.* ◦ **EMPHASIZE** *reading with consonants and thinking about what will make sense.* ◦ *Talk about phonics casually when it seems* **APPROPRIATE** *as you are reading.* ◦ *Enjoyment in reading is the first* **PRIORITY**.

Choosing the RIGHT BOOK

When finding reading material to share, **SELECT** *with as much* **CARE** *as you do when you put* **FOOD** *into your grocery cart.*

Choosing books is choosing food for the mind.

The books you select are very important. A book worthy of reading will be one that you, as an adult, can enjoy. You will find the art delightful, the characters loveable, the contents interesting, instructive or just plain fun!

A good rule of thumb is to choose books which reflect the fact that both the author and the illustrator have spent time creating the best product possible.

Learning is cooperative. One of the best ways to explore an idea together is through a book. The dialogue inspired by a book is as important as the book itself. A good book will stimulate enjoyable discussions. Children need to look at books as a source of pleasure.

It is important to own some cherished books, friends that can be revisited often. But you must also breeze through a large number of books, some of which will be rejected because they are too difficult or uninteresting. Visits to the library are essential!

I asked one mother if she took her six-year-old daughter to the library. She replied that they had lots of books at home. I'm sure they do, but our brains thrive on novelty and freshness. Fresh books are as important as fresh vegetables.

The students I work with usually don't want to read the same book twice. With some information books we read only a page or two each session, especially if they are difficult. Sometimes I pick a paragraph and we practice it a few times so that my reader can hear himself reading fluently.

Make available a constant supply of fresh material on a variety of interesting topics. Read easy books alternately with ones which require more concentration.

There are so many wonderful books available that you don't need to waste valuable time on ones that aren't satisfying. Pick books with expressive words and well-written sentences. There should also be a good balance of short and long words.

Examine the content. The subject matter should be appropriate for the age level. Build as much background as possible before starting to read. Read aloud and discuss difficult passages before the reader attempts them so she can approach the text with understanding. Use illustrations for enjoyment and information but when reading begins her eyes must remain on the print for fluency and comprehension to occur. Pictures enhance understanding but seldom help to read an individual word.

Some reading programs would have you believe that illustrations give children too many clues and make reading easy. How ridiculous! Illustrations do not replace text! I am a firm believer in the value of exposing children to fine art and I love beautiful books. I choose books with attractive illustrations and well-written text for my readers. Take advantage of the amazingly beautiful fiction and non-fiction books available for young people today.

It is possible to discuss, even with young children, the uniqueness of each artist's style or the different ways in which wolves, trees and people are depicted. Discussion based on illustrations builds the worlds of experience so crucial to reading.

The amount of print on each page should be a consideration. Inexperienced readers are uneasy if the page has too much print. I like books that have a small amount of information about one thing on each page. With this format, we quickly arrive at something to discuss.

Choose materials that interest you both. In the beginning, follow the reader's interest. But remember — it is the coach's role to expand experience by introducing new subjects for discussion. Children don't always have to read about dinosaurs, sports, trucks or other current fascinations. I find it exciting when both my reader and I learn something new and it is a delightful treat to discover books that let us laugh together. Engage in stimulating conversations around interesting books and together you will develop a relationship that will make practicing enjoyable.

CONTENT IS IMPORTANT

Texts that are based on a phonics approach to reading often have stories that don't make much sense. They read much like this:

This is a rug.

This is mud.

The rug is in the mud.

The mud is in the sun.

I hit the rug.

The rug is fun.

Is the rug in the mud?

Is the mud in the sun?

Is the rug fun?

In the early days of reading instruction in North America, the first reading text students encountered contained real stories with interesting words and plots. The subject matter was not chosen for simplicity or made up to practice phonics. A page from an old primer illustrates the worthwhile content and complex sentences that beginners were presented with in their first reading book.

The Phonics Primer, Alexander Reading Series, 1915.

Here is a spider. He is in his web. See how fat he is! He must have eaten a great many flies to make him so fat.

He spins a pretty round web, and then says, "Come, little fly, come into my web!"

But if the little fly is wise, he will not listen to the spider's sweet words, for he would never come out of the web again, and would soon be a little dead fly.

CHILDREN NEED REAL LITERATURE

In these early primers, children were introduced to reading through stories that made sense. The content represented a familiar world. Words were chosen to communicate ideas, not to teach sounds.

Sometimes beginning readers are given the most difficult text to read — small words chosen to fit small people! Words are strung together to repeat the sounds being taught. They have to be decoded individually because the story doesn't make sense.

Big words are often more phonetically regular and easier to read than little words and they are certainly a lot more interesting. It's impossible to just use the consonants to make sense when the content is meaningless.

You will be surprised at how readers exceed your expectations when they focus on understanding rather than on memorizing letter combinations and sounding out words. Always use material well above what your reader can read by himself. You are the coach. You are there to help. Many of the common words will be familiar. The tough words will provide opportunity to practice the strategies presented in this book.

Until he is able to read with some fluency, don't ask your child to read alone from books which have not already been shared. Young readers can quickly become discouraged. They practice bad habits such as sounding out every letter and wild guessing.

When your child was learning to walk, you didn't let him struggle on his own and fall down. You provided support for as long as it was needed. Even after he became a competent walker, he still liked to hold your hand on a walk. So it is with reading. Continue to read with your young charges for as long as they need it and enjoy it!

The fondest memory I have from my school days is of the teacher reading from a chapter book every afternoon. Caught up in the excitement of the story, we would beg for just one more chapter. It was so difficult to wait until tomorrow!

Stories transported me from our small town on the prairies to the far corners of the earth. I became acquainted with pirates and kings. I visited Heidi in the mountains of Switzerland where we shared bread and cheese and fresh goat's milk. I can't bring myself to view the movie version. I don't want to erase the scenes still vivid in my imagination.

My uncle talks about his love for the tales of Peter Rabbit. He says he read them hundreds of times. He became a self-educated man through his devotion to reading. Peter Rabbit can take the credit!

My editor told me she had a big, old, illustrated dictionary when she was young. It had colored pictures of fish and birds, etc. It was one of the best investments her parents ever made. Terry spent many hours moving from the illustrations to new words on other pages. Her parents helped her with the tough ones, but the important part was that she remembered the words she discovered on her own. She told the librarian she wanted to be a volcanologist when she grew up! As a college instructor, Terry still uses an illustrated dictionary and still likes volcanoes.

Loving even one book can influence a lifetime. Buy your children beautiful books. Take them to browse in the best bookstores in town. Some hardcover books will be expensive — but worth it! Excellent, inexpensive soft cover editions make books affordable for all.

The best educational investment you can make for your children is in books that they love and enjoy. Compare the amount of money you spend on reading material with your spending on toys, sports equipment and treats. How you choose to spend your money gives a message about what you value!

Taste in books is as distinctive as taste in food. Don't force children to finish books they don't like. This means that you should have a lot of books at hand. Visit the library regularly. While the child picks out books, mom and dad can find material to use for coaching sessions on subjects that interest them. This new information will not only enrich the child's pool of knowledge but it can motivate them to expand their reading to new topics. An added benefit is that reading and talking together about something the coach enjoys builds common understanding and positive relationships. You get to know each other better.

Summary of **K**ey **P O I N T S**

The book you **CHOOSE** *will make a difference.*

Library visits are **CRITICAL**. *Discussion based on illustrations builds* **EXPERIENCE**.

Use books to **STIMULATE** *interesting dialogue.*

Small words are often more **DIFFICULT** *to read than big words.* *Don't ask a beginner to read* **ALONE** *at first.* *Continue to read to children even after they have* **LEARNED** *to read.* **LOVING** *one book can interest a child in books* **FOREVER**.

Handling

F R U S T R A T I O N

Turn your **FRUSTRATION** *into* **JOY**. *Plan fun* **ACTIVITIES** *around books to create* **EXCITEMENT** *about reading.*

To teach, we must explore and notice things together.

▭ Life is busy and full of problems. When children are learning to read or are not reading successfully, we worry about their progress. If they are not reading by the end of grade one, worry can turn into despair. Young readers sense your disappointment and lack of confidence in their ability. They get discouraged and may be reluctant to read to you. The temptation is to lecture about the importance of reading or to punish them by restricting TV or play time. Don't!

This is a critical time in your child's educational career. Her view of herself as a reader is at stake. Avoid getting into a struggle or a shouting match over reading. Attitude and emotional health are more important to reading than anything else at this stage. She doesn't need reprimanding — she needs to discover the fun of books and reading.

Don't ask her to read to you at all for a while. Give her time to regain her confidence. She doesn't want to be embarrassed before her family. Increase the time spent reading to her and spend more time talking and creating things together.

I told one teacher about the book I was writing. She asked me to share this experience with my readers. When her own boy was in grade one he refused to read to her. She became frustrated. But she didn't want to do anything that might turn him off reading. She just continued to read to him and expanded their sharing to include newspapers, magazines, and a variety of other written material. She believed that he would come to reading in his own time.

Ryan began to read in grade two and was soon anxious to read to anyone who would listen! He had been given support at home and time to take advantage of instruction at school. Ryan is now a successful reader who loves to read.

Children don't need lectures about reading, they need to discover that it's enjoyable. The time set aside for reading should strengthen your relationship with your reader. Your primary task is to provide encouragement and to transmit a love for reading.

Creating an environment in which learners feel free to take risks will reduce tension and frustration. When you are both relaxed and have enjoyed some activities together, reading will be more successful. He will be more willing to try when he is not worried about letting you down.

A confident reader is a reader who is permitted to make mistakes. Opportunity must be provided to explore, fail, adjust and recoup without criticism. Read together with good humor, respect for the reader and without regard to timetables.

Conversation is a most important learning tool. Talk, talk, talk with your child about things that you know, have read in books or are questioning yourself. If you both become interested in a subject, look for more information. Read highlights from this material aloud. Simpler books on the same subject can then be read more easily by your child.

For instance, choose a book that involves a scientific concept. Check the date of publication to see if it is current. Get an older or a newer book to find out if the information has changed. Take a trip to a science center or a planetarium. Read a biography about one of your child's heroes to stimulate interest in books about famous people. Extend your reading to include a wide range of topics.

This cannot start too early! We tie together our experiences by reflecting on and combining ideas. Connect what you are reading to other books or to real life experiences. Think of people you know who are like the characters or animals in a story. Be creative! Do everything you can to make reading interesting! You will be rewarded by the sparkle in your reader's eyes.

Progress in reading is directly related to the time invested just as it is for swimming, hockey or knitting. But the world will not come to an end if you do not read every day. If you are tired, out of sorts, in a hurry or just reading to cover a prescribed number of pages, don't! Have a snack. Lie down for a few minutes. Get in the right frame of mind to spend pleasurable time together. Whether reading time is five minutes or an hour, both reader and coach should come away feeling successful.

A full day at school can be tiring and frustrating for students. Don't get in a rut. Sometimes, simply talk about an interesting topic, make a picture, take a walk or do something else you both enjoy.

The choice of books becomes even more important when you and your child are struggling. Choose storybooks where the art is exquisite, the story is short, and the words are strong and expressive. When the story becomes familiar to your reader he will feel comfortable reading sentences and then entire pages by himself. Tasting success is rewarding and it instills the confidence needed to attempt longer stories.

Approach reading in a light-hearted, joyful manner with the same confidence and spirit of fun that you had when your child was learning to walk and talk. Lighten up! Five minutes of shared enjoyment is better than thirty minutes of, "Let's get this over with so we can get on with our day!"

IDEAS TO GET YOU STARTED

I have a wonderful collection of original books made by children. Creating a book and sharing it with others is one of the best ways I have found to generate interest in reluctant readers. I save cloth scraps, used gift wrap and greeting cards, anything that might be used for collages. Images from children's wallpaper books, available at your local hardware store, inspire ideas for stories. Wallpaper samples are especially good because you can make books quickly and have a large collection in a short time.

Encourage children to develop different artistic styles by having available a variety of paints, pastels and other art supplies. They love to copy the styles of artists from their favorite books. Barbara Reid and Eric Carle are good examples. Making books is fun. Reading their own creations to others is a remarkable confidence booster!

Write your most treasured family stories from both the past and present. Your child will love reading them. These can become increasingly complex as the child's skill grows. Make original books about some of the stories. A scrap book filled with these anecdotes will become a family treasure.

Use a tape recorder to introduce variety into your sharing time. When you have finished reading, the child can retell the story on tape using his own words. Or you can stop before the end of a story to let the child create his own ending. Print out taped material and use it for reading. This is a great way to get reluctant readers started.

Retelling is also a valuable way to strengthen comprehension skills. Children who learn to visualize and make pictures in their heads store information in long term memory more efficiently. Assume the roles of characters in the story you have just read. Create conversations they might have had. Be an object in the story, e.g. the forest or baby's chair in *Goldilocks* and tell the story from another point of view. Tape the new version and use it for reading material or as the text for another book.

My daughter's family went on a trip when their son, Sean, was quite young. When they returned, she sequenced the pictures in an album and left it on the coffee table for him to look at. It became a favorite and he still remembers the trip. He also developed a fascination for pictures and photo albums. Photos can serve as the illustrations for a book about your vacation.

HELPERS ARE NEEDED

Many of these activities need the support of an adult or older child. Have fun with them so that they don't become just another chore. Co-author the book so that it is a joint effort. You contribute whatever is needed to make a product that you can both be proud of. If it's not fun and the child doesn't buy into it, postpone the activity and come to it from another way on another day!

Reading is its own reward. Resist the temptation to give treats, money or bicycles for progress in reading. A reward not gained is seen as a failure. You are communicating a subtle message: if you would just try harder you could do it. The child may already be giving his best effort. Your role is to provide encouragement.

CELEBRATING READING

If there is a tape available to accompany a book, have the child listen to it before you read together. After hearing the story, you will be surprised at how much of the text he can read by himself.

Ask your child to create a story based on the pictures in a book. You can tape it or just tell it for fun.

Teach your child how to ask good questions. Then have him question you about such things as the artist's style, the strengths and weaknesses of a story and so on.

Invite a friend (young or old) to bring some reading material and to share in your reading time.

In a special journal, make a *Books Shared Record*. Record the names of books shared, author, date and interesting comments. Many children love to copy so the entries might be done with a minimum of help. Include the books you read to the child in the record.

▭ If you have grandparents or friends who are regular visitors, develop a routine where they look at new entries in the *Books Shared Record* and ask questions about any of the books listed. A sticker or signature can be used to indicate where to begin on the next visit.

▭ Have your child dictate or write a letter to someone telling about a book or an activity. He might write about the ways he sees himself improving as a reader.

▭ Help your child write a book for a younger sibling or a friend, telling them how to read. An original book would be a great gift for grandma and grandpa.

▭ If you have a video camera, create a documentary about reading. Tape a pretend interview with an author. Film an original play based on a favorite story. All members of the family can join in on the fun. Older kids especially like to do this. The video camera is an underused teaching tool!

▭ Use clay or play dough to create the setting and characters from one of your stories. Make a cardboard backdrop and you will have a delightful display.

▭ Puppets are fun to use when telling a story. You could video tape your performance. Libraries have books on how to make both simple and complex puppets. Read them together!

Your child will build skills in many areas by engaging in these activities and you will discover your hidden talents, too!

A story is told about a woman who asked Einstein how to help her son excel in mathematics. Einstein told her to stretch his imagination and to teach him the great myths of the past. We must find ways to keep alive the creative imagination that is so evident in young children. Reading takes place in the imagination.

Summary of Key POINTS

Overcome frustration by creating **FUN** *activities.*
⬦ *Help children to* **EXPLORE** *and* **NOTICE**
things. ⬦ *Resist putting too much pressure on*
beginners. ⬦ *Above all else, make* **SHARING**
times **ENJOYABLE**. ⬦ *Create a relaxed environment*
so that a child can take risks without fear
of criticism. ⬦ **CELEBRATE** *reading through*
enjoyable activities. ⬦ *Let schools teach*
reading while you keep **CONFIDENCE** *and*
DESIRE *alive.* ⬦ *Reading is its own* **REWARD**!

Adolescents

AN**D** **A**DULT**S**

Poor readers can learn to read **FLUENTLY**

and **CONFIDENTLY** *with the help of an*

informed, supportive **COACH**.

Combining sense and sound for effective reading.

▭ Bryce was in a grade two French immersion class. One day he asked me if I would like him to teach me French. I said that was a great idea. He painstakingly printed the forms of the verb "to be" and other words, which he had me carefully pronounce. The next time he came to visit I suggested that we carry on with another lesson. When we got out the sheet he had written on he looked up and said, "Grandma, I think I've taught you everything I know!"

When I considered adding a chapter to my original book I felt a lot like Bryce — perhaps I had written everything I know about learning to read simply and naturally. However, as I reflected over the ten years since I wrote the book, I began to realize how profoundly my approach to reading has helped many of the adults who bring children to my private consultations. As I explain the reading process, a light goes on for these adults. They suddenly realize why they don't like to read. For them reading is too slow. They have to go back and re-read much of the material to get meaning. Many have later told me how their reading improved as they coached their children.

I also began to reflect on the older children I had worked with over the years. Adolescents who have failed to learn to read well are in an especially critical situation. It is difficult to find new ways to help them. Money for reading is, more and more, being spent on early literacy. Over the years, adolescent non-readers have had a lot of teaching but it hasn't worked, so more of the same is not a solution.

Teens who do not read effectively have had repeated failures in reading and writing — for six or more years. A sense of despair has set in. At the end of one of my reading presentations a distraught mother came up to me. She said that her thirteen-year-old daughter, a non-reader, felt so ashamed and inferior to her peers that she had tried to commit suicide.

A teacher in high school told me another story that illustrates this point. A girl in her class was reading at a grade two level. But when it was time for the class to do silent reading, she would choose a book by Shakespeare in an attempt to keep her peers from knowing that she couldn't read.

A concerned grandmother told me how her thirteen-year-old grandson pretends to read the menu, always ordering what someone else has ordered to hide his embarrassment at being unable to read.

Those who don't read as well as their peers may exhibit serious behavior problems — they become bullies, clowns or introverts. Especially during the teenage years, the basic need to feel accepted and important is huge — an over-arching human need, and teens fulfill it in whatever ways they can.

Heartened by these insights, I decided to write this new chapter. It is aimed specifically at adults who don't read as well as they would like, and at parents who have older children with reading difficulties.

A DIFFICULT TIME OF CHANGE

Adolescents are experiencing biological, cognitive and social change at an accelerated rate. They may exhibit mood swings and inconsistent behavior. There is peer pressure not to appear too academic and they want to be cool around their peers. They are pulling away from parents, so they don't take advice well. Those who don't read well have learned to avoid reading, and they have built up defense mechanisms that must be dismantled.

Sometimes we refer to these students as "reluctant readers." I think it would be more appropriate to refer to them as "discouraged readers" because the following conditions have not been met:

They haven't discovered the delight and fun of reading.

They can't read well enough to read the books their friends are reading.

They have never had good grades because they can't read the textbooks or test questions.

Poor readers create stories they tell themselves so they can cope with failure. Those who work with them, both parents and professionals, may have given them labels that they use as excuses. An indifferent attitude toward reading has become embedded. They have to shed the labels and change their focus if they are to become readers.

PRIDE AND FEAR

Someone who attended Alcoholics Anonymous told me that two main things keep people from dealing with their problems — pride and fear. The herd instinct, the need to belong and to have friends, the absolute necessity of not standing out from one's peers, is especially huge for kids from twelve to sixteen.

To fulfill this need it is necessary to put on a brave face in public, one that really doesn't represent how they feel or how they view themselves inside. A friend who works with both adults and teens made an interesting comment. She noticed that in group situations adults like to find a space to themselves, but teens get as close to each other as possible.

Adolescents who are not able to discuss the current "hot-reads" feel left out of the loop. Many teens deal with this by trying to avoid talking about books or by listening closely to the comments of others and repeating them so they don't have to let their friends know they can't read. Pride can keep teenagers from admitting their problems and from seeking help.

WE ALL FEAR FAILURE

A.A. Milne wrote in *The House At Pooh Corner* about an incident when Pooh and Piglet were walking together in the Hundred Acre Wood.

> Piglet says suddenly, "Look, Pooh! There's something in one of the Pine Trees."
>
> "So there is!" said Pooh, looking up wonderingly. "There's an Animal." Piglet took Pooh's arm, in case Pooh was frightened.

Those who have failed to read well are frightened but, like Piglet, they want to find ways to keep it from showing. They are constantly being told how important reading is. The implication is that if they just tried harder, they could do it. Worrying that they might never be able to read, with all the implications that handicap has for the future, makes it even harder for them. They need an arm that offers reassurance.

Fear plays a debilitating role because they have been taught by so many over the years, yet are still failing. They may not want more remediation because they fear yet another round of failure. They just don't want to deal with another person about something that causes so much pain.

I especially remember handsome, twin boys whose parents brought them for a consult. Their peers were calling them stupid because they had to go to a special class. They were getting into fights as a result. When they got to my house, they didn't want to come in. Their parents finally talked them inside the door, but they stood with their backs to the wall, reluctant to go any further. After we all relaxed a little, they each agreed to read a short piece for me. They sounded out individual words slowly, in a monotone voice. Then I showed them how to read quickly and fluently. I taught their parents how to conduct effective practice sessions. A couple of weeks later they came back, eager to show me how much better they could read already.

Parents need to recognize the role of pride and fear in their adolescents, and to approach any offer of help in a sensitive way. They might say something like, "I know that reading slowly is making it difficult for you to keep up in school. I have found a new book that shows how to read more quickly. Could we read a bit of it together?"

Read chapters two, three and four of this book to show your adolescent that this approach is different. You might agree to a few practice sessions where, together, you experiment with this new approach to reading. That's not a big commitment.

GREG'S STORY

I coached a bright young man who, although unable to read, was successful in his professional sports career. He had been labeled dyslexic in grade two and was shifted into what I call "The Medical Model" for the rest of his school career. He told me he remembers saying to his mother at the beginning of grade four, "Please don't tell anyone about my reading. Just let me be like the other kids this year."

Unfortunately, she couldn't give him his wish. School is about labeling and sorting, and he could not avoid being singled out for the remediation that was so painful. We have to be careful not to blame anyone for what happened to Greg. Everyone who worked with him wanted him to read. They were all doing what they thought was best. I helped Greg define reading in a new way by using hockey as a metaphor. A player can focus on the rules of the game, how he is skating and holding his stick, and on the moves the coach has taught in practice. But effective players focus on the game itself. The mechanics operate at a subconscious level. A hockey coach once said to me, "The last thing I want my players to do is to think about making a mistake or about the techniques of skating or hockey when they are playing the game."

It is the same with reading. Good readers don't agonize over the mechanics of words. They skip over that level of detail and absorb the meaning that is being transmitted by the words.

I gave Greg familiar material to read, and instructed him to just say the consonants as he saw them. If he was paying attention to what the text was saying, most of the time the right word would come into his mind. I modeled what I wanted him to do by quietly saying the consonants for him if he halted. When he stumbled over a word too much, I gave it to him quickly. Anything to keep him reading fluently!

I often pre-read a passage and stopped for him to fill in the next word without seeing the text. He was usually able to do it quite easily. I did this to demonstrate that good readers don't look carefully at every word they read. Their understanding of the subject lets their subconscious mind fill in many of the words. As I helped him to shift his focus from the mechanics of reading to what the text was saying, he was freed from the prison that too much sounding out had constructed in his mind. For the first time, Greg heard himself reading fluently. He exclaimed, "All these years and I didn't understand this!"

FAILURE ERODES CONFIDENCE

For adult and adolescent non-readers, the realization that so much time and effort has been spent in the attempt to help them learn to read only serves to dig deeper ditches of despair. This is especially true if, year after year, the same approach is taken. Eventually, they learn one lesson well — there is something wrong with them. Reading is beyond their grasp.

However, that is rarely true. The problem for many is that bad habits have become entrenched by too much slow and careful reading. The secret of reading is to pass your eye quickly over the words, and to use your knowledge of the subject matter to make meaning based on the fewest possible clues. Anything that stops the reader from quickly carrying on to the next word detracts from meaning. This is why slow readers get discouraged, give up, and seldom read anything of length or substance. They stop so often to figure out words that they lose track of what they have read.

DEFINITION GUIDES INTERVENTION

Let's take my work with Greg as an example of how to help adolescents and adults with reading difficulties. Greg had to have someone sit beside him to force him to read quickly and with minimal clues, focusing on meaning. He had to forget all the strategies that he had learned over many years of reading instruction. The sound-it-out mentality that he was executing to a fault when he first read for me — stopping before every long word to figure it out, and carefully considering each word in turn — had to be abandoned. His focus had to be redirected from 'reading is figuring out words' to 'reading is making sense of text.'

Sounding each letter or combination of letters in a word often leads to what I call wild guessing. By the time these readers get to the end of the word they have forgotten how it started. They just make a wild guess, based on the consonants they remember, and keep going. When readers do this, they do not have the right definition of reading. As a coach, you'll know you are making progress when your reader stops when the text doesn't make sense.

If you believe, as this book argues, that reading is not accomplished until the reader makes sense of what is being read, then you must approach the coaching process from that point of view. If, however, you believe that reading is about figuring out words, then you will want to place your emphasis, as too often happens with well-meaning reading coaches both in and out of the schools, on practicing the rules for sounding out.

"I'M READING GOOD. I'M IMPRESSED WITH MYSELF."

This comment by Jason, one of my young readers, contains the secret of success. Jason had to be able to label himself as a reader. He had to hear himself reading meaningful material fluently enough so that he could define it as reading. For most children this happens quite naturally, but for those who get hooked on the mechanics of reading it may not happen quickly enough, before they become discouraged.

Margaret Meek, my mentor, says it well in her book *Learning to Read*. "If your child wants to read, and can't, then he needs collaborative help to learn. The trouble is he may be having reading lessons, which are not always the same thing. He needs to experience success so he can see himself getting better, not worse."

STEPS TO SUCCESS

The learner must want to learn. Some students whose parents bring them for help have already decided they are finished with reading. I am unable to work with those students. We cannot cross the threshold of another's mind — we all have to engage in our own learning. The whole process stops when we can't interest the reader in expending the effort to try again.

A coach has to be found. This could be a parent or older sibling. However, sometimes relationships in the family break down after too many failed attempts at reading — older students simply may not want to work with family anymore. In that case, you must find someone willing to commit the time and effort to act as coach. It may be possible to find a friend or a peer to help. You may want to pay them for the time they commit.

The coach has to be willing to learn. He or she has to be willing to become familiar with the approach to reading advocated in this book, and to adopt its philosophy. The coach has to refrain from teaching any strategies that involve breaking words apart. There are only two parts to reading — print and experience. You want someone who will focus on building experience and making meaning, who will help your reader bring his innate knowledge to the task of reading, the way all good readers do.

There must be no testing. This approach is based on viewing reading as an enjoyable activity. Interesting reading material not related to grade level is used, so there is no need for testing. For fluent reading to happen readers must be able to relax, without fear of judgment. In this context, mistakes are a learning opportunity, not a reason to pass judgment.

Set up a schedule. Coach and learner have to spend time together. This may be difficult. It may mean giving up other activities for a while. The good news is that adolescents have learned a lot in school and they know everything they need to know to read well. They often just don't know how to put it together. In my experience, when they learn how to change focus, most of them soon become fluent readers of subject matter to which they can bring some understanding.

Choice of reading material is critical. Use age and interest level as your criteria. Material with strong sentences and a rich vocabulary gives you something to work with. Start with a familiar subject and progress into new topics. I have listed some additional books in the Bibliograpy that I like to use. They have a wide variety of interesting subjects to explore with short paragraphs to use for practicing speed and fluency. I avoid using fiction because it is difficult to build background for words and ideas that will be encountereed.

Talk before reading. Engage in lots of dialogue about the subject being read, and about the new words that will be encountered. Doing this in advance sets the stage by helping learners bring prior experience with the subject matter to the text. Examine diagrams and illustrations. It is not cheating to read difficult passages aloud before asking them to read. The goal is to make it easy to succeed.

Stock up on words. The concepts around words are the keys to making sense. Jot down unfamiliar words as you discuss them. Give the list to your reader at the end of each session. He then writes the words, with their meanings, on index cards. This makes them easy to review until he owns them and can use them in both reading and writing. Start each session by asking him for the meaning of a few of them as a review. Words are the building blocks of thought. Good readers have a plentiful supply.

Tips for independent reading. Have a dictionary handy when reading difficult material. Read the beginning and ending sentences of the paragraph first. Skim-read the paragraph as quickly as possible. Put a check mark beside unfamiliar words. Look up their meanings and add them to your index cards. Write a question about the paragraph to focus your mind on making meaning. Read the paragraph again. Choose a sentence to turn into a question. It takes understanding of the content to frame questions. If it is study material, write a summary sentence to put in your outline notes.

FOSTERING CHANGE

We cannot change what we cannot see. The only way we can change is to have a clear idea of what we are doing now, see another way that makes sense, and find a method of implementing the change. We have to forget the past, move beyond blaming anyone or any set of circumstances for our failure, and be willing to implement the new plan. Reading is always about making sense of text.

Summary of **K**ey P O I N T S

Choose interesting materials with **STRONG** *words.* ❋ **DICTIONARIES** *are bedfellows of readers.* ❋ *Time spent in dialogue is the secret.* ❋ **TACT** *and* **PATIENCE** *are essential qualities.* ❋ *All ages have to begin again and learn to behave like a reader.* ❋ **FLUENCY** *is a feeling.* ❋ *Alice's advice,* *"Take care of the* **SENSE** *and the* **SOUNDS** *will take care of themselves."*

Summary SUMMARY

The greatest **GIFT** *you can give your* **CHILD** *is a* **QUESTIONING** *mind that has been taught a variety of ways to find* **ANSWERS** *to life's* **CHALLENGES**.

Helping another to become a reader requires time, effort and patience.

No amount of force can open the door to another's mind. The key is on the inside.

We want aspiring readers to feel successful so they can praise themselves and talk to themselves as readers. Minimizing the attention paid to mistakes and looking for opportunities to focus attention on successful performance will help achieve this goal. Whatever you do, protect their self-image. Help them to save face.

I emphasize again the essential role that experience, housed in each unique pool of knowledge, plays in reading. Students become more effective readers if the emphasis is always on building experience before reading.

Create a comfortable reading environment making it safe to take risks. Challenge readers with a variety of materials, stimulating a love for reading. People who experience the joy of reading choose to spend time with books.

You may have serious concerns about your child's progress. You know better than anyone how your child is doing. If you sense a problem developing, keep in close contact with the teacher but do not discuss it with the child. Remember, if he picks up on your uncertainty and becomes discouraged, the teacher's job will be more difficult.

Society has shaped our attitudes about learning to read by treating reading as a skill to be taught to children when they go to school. I view reading as an art. Teaching and instruction are important to learning an art, but there are many subjective things that can only be learned by working beside an artist. Reading treated as a skill makes it a duty to be performed. Reading treated as an art makes it a pleasure to be enjoyed.

I have shared with you my understanding of reading and some of my experiences with aspiring readers and their parents. I hope the views presented in this book will make your role as a reading coach even more special and enjoyable.

A story is told of the great pianist Paderewski who was performing at Carnegie Hall. When Paderewski left the piano at intermission, a young boy climbed on the stage, sat down at the piano and began to play chopsticks. The audience was aghast at the young fellow's impudence. Paderewski turned around and came back to the piano. Sitting down beside the boy, he began to play chopsticks with him.

Combine your talents. Together you will create a better performance.

Bibliography BOOKLIST

Carroll, Lewis, (1983). *Alice in Wonderland.* Grosset & Dunlap

Meek, M., (1982). *Learning to Read.* London: Bodley Head

Milne, A.A., (1988). *The House At Pooh Corner.* New York: Dutton

Ulderico, G. (1994). *The Rainbow Goblins.* New York: Thames and Hudson

REFERENCES FOR SERIES BOOKS

The following series are examples of the kind of materials I use for my coaching sessions. They have varying levels of difficulty and a variety of topics, some of which are listed.

DK Google e Guides Series. Dorling Kindersley and Google ™

Earth • Mummy • Space Travel • Encyclopedia

Eyewitness Guides. Dorling Kindersley

Ancient Civilizations • Sports • Electronics • Science • History
A wonderful series with many other subjects.

Eye Wonder. Dorling Kindersley

Big Cats • Bugs • Dinosaurs • Ocean • Reptiles • Birds

DK Guides. Dorling Kindersley

Space • Weather • Ocean • Mammals

Let's Read and Find Out. Harper Collins

Mars • International Space Station • What is the moon like?

Superguides. Dorling Kindersley

Ballet • Soccer • Gymnastics • Ice Skating • Martial Arts
• Swimming • Tennis • Riding

You will never think the same way about words and how to make sense of language again!

Vera has been given a special gift — the ability to communicate simply and clearly. Her exuberant energy, natural sense of humor and timely stories add the spice necessary to ensure memorable presentations. Vera has spoken to many educators, parents, volunteers, women's groups and conferences on education and motivational topics.

COMMENTS FROM PARTICIPANTS:

* Very hands-on, practical information.

* Honesty, open discussion of issues and very informative.

* Please have her back — many parents could benefit.

* Excellent speaker. I really learned new ideas.

Vera Goodman's wisdom, unique insights and ability to engage the audience guarantees a great learning experience for everyone. Vera is unique and fascinating — she is definitely one of a kind!

Ask Vera to tailor a presentation to your needs today.

Website: www.readingwings.com
E-mail: info@readingwings.com
Toll-Free: **1-800-411-9660**

"Vera informed and entertained our audience consistently."

Margaret Reid – *Principal*

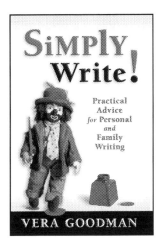

SiMPlY Write!

Practical Advice *for* Personal *and* Family Writing

Make writing an enjoyable part of your life. You, and everyone in your family, can use writing to strengthen relationships and to extend thinking and imagination.

This ground-breaking book presents simple ways to give writing a more central place in your own life and in that of your family. Children become writers when the adults in their lives model and celebrate writing. Learn how parents and teachers can work together in partnership to promote writing and raise strong writers.

When writing is celebrated, students benefit by choosing to use writing to become more self-confident, thoughful, creative and curious.

Everyone who reads this book will feel inspired to start writing

Vera Goodman's lifelong commitment to help struggling readers find pleasure and meaning in reading led her to create Reading Wings, a unique coaching program focusing on the experiences and enjoyment that coaches and students share as they learn together. Vera has taken her distinctive coaching style and cutting-edge strategies to a wide variety of audiences. Her vivacious personality and sparkling energy have endeared her to thousands of people who have been influenced by her bestselling first book, *Reading is More than Phonics!* (now re-published as *Simply Read!*), or by her dynamic presentations and powerful teaching video, *Coaching Young Readers.*

As a teacher, administrator, conference speaker and workshop facilitator for many years, Vera is recognized as a leading authority in teaching children and adults how to become competent and enthusiastic readers. In her latest book, *Simply Write!*, she shares inspiring stories, common-sense tips and delightful insights into writing for all ages.

Vera's work was celebrated by Global Television in 2003 when she received the Woman of Vision award for her contributions to literacy. Recently she was honored by Seattle Pacific University, her alma mater, with the Medallion Award for excellence and outstanding service in her field. On graduating from Central Collegiate High School in Moose Jaw, Saskatchewan, she received the Governor General's Medal for scholarship. She has an MA in language arts from the University of Calgary.

Vera has three daughters. She lives in Calgary, Alberta, Canada, where she spends as much time as possible with her three grandchildren. One of her hobbies is riding her horse, Missy, in the foothills.

Printed in the United States
By Bookmasters